Robert's Rules of Order

A Comprehensive Guide to Robert's Rules of Order

John Cummings

Table of Contents

Introduction 1

Chapter One: Robert's Rules of Order (RRO) – History and Background 4

Chapter Two: What is the Deliberative Assembly? 11

Chapter Three: About Meetings 23

Chapter Four: Conducting Business the RRO Way 34

Chapter Five: Everything You Need to Know About Motions 41

Chapter Six: Participating Courteously and Objectively in Debates..53

Chapter Seven: All About Voting 60

Chapter Eight: Implementing RRO in a Meeting 71

Final Words 78

Introduction

Living in a society that adheres to democratic principles demands a unique way of communicating and transacting that is just and fair compared to other forms of governance. As individuals, we enjoy inalienable rights but are also responsible for inescapable duties that demonstrate how responsible we are when living together.

Our conduct with each other - a duty that we have to perform without question - measures how we maintain order collectively. This is just as true in situations where we have to conduct business as part of any organization. Going about business without structure or proper procedures in place will result in complete anarchy.

Is this a good thing? Obviously not. Even if the universe seeks to introduce chaos at every turn, order is necessary for every walk of life. In fact, it is twice as bad for business, just as the absence of social order reflects poorly on a democracy. Speaking of which, the effectiveness with which organizations conduct business depends on rules created, documented, and adhered to by its members and elected officers.

Also known as parliamentary procedure, it accounts for every member's actions in the organization and ensures that the decisions made are for the "greater good." Interpreted as laws that are part of a reference book, these guidelines ensure that every member of the said organization gets to speak and vote – as is expected in a democracy.

But why should any organization adopt a parliamentary procedure for the sake of conducting business? It's a fair question to ask.

If anything, these rules ensure that all business conducted runs smoothly and efficiently by following time-tested and proven principles. To use an everyday metaphor, it's just like following the rules of the road that result in the unrestricted flow of traffic. To not follow the rules – in either case – would result in delays and even utter disaster. In short, following these rules means that you can have productive meetings where things get done in a timely and ordered manner.

But there's more: not only is the organization's purpose fulfilled by conducting business in a just and courteous manner, but this is also done in such a way that everyone feels heard. Overall, these written procedures are widely considered the best possible method by which organizations can make decisions on a variety of simple and complex questions and take every member's point of view seriously.

So, if you are part of an organization looking for a framework of rules by which to conduct business at meetings in such a manner, it would be wise to look at parliamentary procedure available for this very purpose. Robert's Rules of Order serves as an excellent starting point, even if it can be quite lengthy to go through.

This book draws on the broad framework of rules outlined in Robert's Rules of Order to help organizations grasp the main points necessary to establish and adhere to their own rules of order. Yes, it should come as a relief that you don't have to follow every guideline expanded upon, but you can tweak these rules to suit your organization's needs. This makes sense since the creation of the first edition of Robert's Rules of Order was almost a hundred years ago, even if nearly every rule in his book can prove to be just as relevant in this day and age.

But before we do this, it's wise to gain some context on the creation and development of Robert's Rules of Order before we jump into the following chapters that can help us conduct meetings in a timely, ordered, and productive manner.

With that said, we will look at the humble beginnings of parliamentary procedure in England to its adoption for the drafting of the state and federal constitutions in the United States in the first chapter. We will also cover information found in the earliest "manuals" that shed light on parliamentary law and the events leading to this book's compilation on parliamentary law. Finally, we will look at Henry M. Robert III's work that can help organizations – government or otherwise – function efficiently.

Chapter One: Robert's Rules of Order (RRO) – History and Background

Parliamentary Law – Humble Beginnings

Parliamentary law, in its current form, owes much to the formation of the English Parliament. Going as far back as the thirteenth century, the need for parliamentary procedures became a priority when the House of Commons and the House of Lords was first formed. Yet, the idea of putting down these procedures in writing for future reference would only materialize in the sixteenth century. Still, if one must list a starting point for all things pertaining to parliamentary law, English Parliament was the first to recognize the need for such a list of rules and the need to document it for the benefit of its members.

The first book on parliamentary law was written by Sir Thomas Smyth in the 1560s and was titled Le Republica: The Manner on Gouvernement or Policy of the Realme of England. G. Petit also wrote a smaller version titled Lex Parliamentaria in 1689 and which helped many first-time parliamentarians become acquainted with how business was conducted in English Parliament. It should be noted that a lot of principles outlined and explained in these two books remain just as relevant today. Even then, the officially recognized version of parliamentary law was penned as entries in the Journal of the House of Commons.

The Adoption of Parliamentary Law in the United States

With the founding of numerous colonies in the United States in the seventeenth century, the need for self-government became a reality. As a result, the parliamentary procedure made its way across the Atlantic in 1619 when adopted by the very first representative assembly known as the House of Burgesses in the Colony of Virginia. As history would have it, a number of new colonies would spring up in quick succession. Their representative assemblies would go on to tweak and use these parliamentary rules to conduct business in an orderly fashion. With its origins in the English Parliament, parliamentary law found a new home, so to speak, in the New World.

Since these parliamentary rules offered order and efficiency when it came to decision-making, the drafting of state constitutions was easy despite being very different. Also, these same rules obtained from the English Parliament were used to take decisive action against the British Empire in the events building up to the American Revolution. Specifically, it was the Second Continental Congress that was able to declare war on the British swiftly while also being able to draft the Declaration of Independence and the United States Constitution by carefully considering both the voice of the majority along with the rights of the minority.

Despite these general benefits of parliamentary law, there was still much confusion since one state legislature's rules were different from the next. The codification of parliamentary law into a single, comprehensive document for organizations of all types was the need of the hour. It would take another 100 years for this to materialize, thanks to Henry M. Robert's book titled Robert's Rules of Order, but two other authors would attempt such a feat and which are worth mentioning here.

The Thomas Jefferson Manual

After the American Revolution brought liberty to the United States, it was Thomas Jefferson, serving as Vice-President of the United States and as the Presiding Officer of the Senate, who felt the need to codify the rules followed by parliament concerning decision-making, debates, votes, and appeals. At that time, each branch of Congress had been asked to form its own rules on how to conduct its daily affairs and which required a constant reference by one and all to a definite system of rules. Unfortunately, this system of rules was not available at that time.

As a result, Jefferson published his book titled Manual of Parliamentary Practice in 1801 and in which he expresses his indebtedness to John Hatsell's work. The latter was a clerk in the House of Commons who published a book on eighteenth-century parliamentary procedure titled Precedents of Proceedings in the House of Commons in 1781.

History remembers Thomas Jefferson as being the first American author to publish an authoritative work on parliamentary procedure. Without a doubt, he was the first to recognize the need for rules and a degree of uniformity when conducting business in all branches of government in the United States. It wouldn't be long before many state legislatures and other organizations would adopt this manual as an authoritative work on the subject of parliamentary rules. Also, while the Senate would adopt this manual, the House of Representatives would codify their own set of rules and practices as a replacement for Jefferson's seminal work in the area of parliamentary law.

The Cushing Manual

At the time when the Cushing Manual was written, parliamentary law had been adopted by legislative bodies. Its author, Luther S. Cushing, who was the Clerk at the Massachusetts House of Representatives, wanted to create a set of rules of non-legislative bodies as well. Apart from political bodies, rules for decision-making were also necessary for cultural, scientific, charitable, and scientific organizations even if the conditions in which they operated were different from that of legislative bodies.

So, to meet the needs of many voluntary societies in the United States, the Cushing Manual was written and published in 1845. In fact, he specifically stated that the procedures outlined in his work were "for assemblies of every description, but more specifically for those who are not legislative in their character." In only putting down "common parliamentary law" in his book, Cushing believed that upon necessity, non-legislative organizations should create and adopt additional rules of order apart from those in his manual.

Despite his best efforts, the manual, being well-received, could not fit the needs of organizations at the time. The goal of creating a system of rules that organizations could use and tweak for their own needs would not be realized until Henry M. Robert attended his first meeting. Speaking of which, his embarrassment at having no knowledge of parliamentary law when presiding over a meeting served as the foundation for the book titled Robert's Rules of Order.

Robert's Rules of Order

After presiding over his first meeting, Robert realized that research on conducting business in a meeting was necessary before he presided over the next meeting. While a small pocketbook gave him a few guidelines for reference, he continued to look for books that offered practical information on parliamentary law.

Some of the books that he read consisted of familiar ones published at home and in England. Jefferson's and Cushing's Manual, Wilson's Digest, the House of Representatives' Rules, and Barclay's Digest of Rules and Practices of the House were some of these books. There were differing opinions on several parliamentary rules and, on the whole, served as a hindrance to anyone who wanted to acquire knowledge on parliamentary law.

Still, despite these differences, Robert decided to put down a parliamentary manual that would borrow the general principles from the rules and practice of Congress and adapt it according to the organization's needs. What Robert envisioned was a book of rules of order that could be adopted easily by any organization but without preventing them from adding any special rules that might be necessary. In other words, if there were a better rule for certain conditions in an organization, then that rule would be adopted instead of adopting all rules from the House, Senate, or other state legislative assemblies in the United States.

With this objective in mind, he would begin writing the 176-page book titled Pocket Manual of Rules of Order for Deliberative Assemblies in 1874 and would finish printing the book by the end of the following year. By February 1876, S.C Griggs & Co. of Chicago would offer Robert a contract hesitantly as the publisher wasn't sure of the demand for such a book. Upon renaming it as Robert's Rules of Order, 3000 copies of the book were sold in four months.

Now, enthusiasm for the book's contents did not diminish over time, resulting in two more editions being published, and by which time, half a million copies had been sold. It wouldn't be long before a complete revision of the book was completed by Henry M. Robert in 1915 and which contained only one-fourth of the content present in the third edition of the book published in 1893. Upon Robert's death in 1923, this work on parliamentary law for deliberative assemblies of all kinds continued to be reworked, refined, and revised based on the numerous questions on parliamentary law that crop up from time to time. As one can tell from the response that this book has received, this work on parliamentary law remains in great demand, despite being written almost a century ago.

Chapter Summary

- Parliamentary law began with procedures documented in English Parliament since the sixteenth century.
- Sir Thomas Smyth and G. Petit wrote two books on parliamentary procedures at the same time.
- Parliamentary law came to the United States upon the formation of the House of Burgesses in the Colony of Virginia.

In the next chapter, you will learn about the deliberative assembly and its workings.

Chapter Two: What is the Deliberative Assembly?

Definition

The term 'deliberative assembly' was first used in 1774 by Edmund Burke in a meeting in Bristol to describe a group of people who meet as equals at an agreed time to discuss and determine a course of action. As Henry Robert discovered, members who gather at these meetings require rules by which arriving at a decision is made with minimal effort. Or else, the presiding officers will have to deal with disorderly conduct and, at the very worst, utter chaos. So, this body of people that common parliamentary law applies to and which, as Henry envisioned, should help in conducting business in an orderly, efficient manner.

Unlike groups of people who attend education seminars, sports events, or music concerts, this group of people attends a specific meeting to attain organizational goals as listed in the governing documents. Called members, the people who participate in this meeting in a designated area, have the freedom to make judgments by voting and abstain from voting altogether. They can vote and make motions and participate in debates as well, thanks to the right extended to them by the organization's bylaws.

If that's not enough, these very members have the right to participate and represent other members who are not present at the meeting. This is only if a quorum exists at such a meeting. Lastly, since every member's vote is considered equal in the decision-making process, the will of the majority will prevail. That said, the minority will also get a chance to have their voice heard before making a final decision on any business.

Structure of the Deliberative Assembly

While a deliberative assembly mostly consists of members, presiding officers such as the President, Vice-President, Secretary, and Treasurer also exist. Each of these officers is elected from among the members themselves and has definite functions to perform in each meeting until they are discharged from that office. One must point out that these officers cannot function as both a member and an officer simultaneously when the assembly is in the process of arriving at a critical decision being discussed.

Among the various officers mentioned, the President and Secretary are considered the most important for the roles they play when conducting business during any deliberative assembly meeting. Lastly, members are appointed, by virtue of their field of expertise, to either a standing or special committee as participants to investigate certain business matters. A committee chairman is also appointed to ensure that the work assigned to the said committee reaches fruition.

Now, there are five primary types of deliberative assemblies where people meet at a particular time and place to conduct business:

(1) the assembly of an organized society

(2) the board

(3) the legislative body

(4) the convention

(5) the mass meeting

While our definition of the deliberative assembly and its composition might be acceptable by common parliamentary law, each organization, being as varied in purpose and structure, might adopt special rules suited to its situation. These rules will be found in the governing documents and will often determine what the order of business is and how it is conducted when said deliberative assembly meets.

Governing Documents

Any organization requires governing documents that provide information about its identity and purpose as well as operations. But what does this have to do with the "deliberative assembly," one might ask? Without these written documents in place, we would not be able to define the roles of members and officers, describe business in its entirety, or even set essential rules that are usually necessary for conducting business in a fair, orderly, and efficient manner.

With that said, let us look at four important documents that will give members and officers adequate information to run an organization and use them when it comes to conducting business in a quick and orderly fashion.

Corporate Charter

For organizations to work as a corporation, the state or federal government must grant it such a status. So, if an organization has been granted such a status, its corporate charter would include the legal name, address, and purpose.

Now, there are reasons why an organization might want to be incorporated with the state. This includes holding property, preparing legally binding contracts, being recognized as an organization, or even protecting its members from liability when they perform the assigned organizational duties.

To carry this out, an attorney who is familiar with state law will be able to help incorporate the organization and where the incorporation papers such as the Articles of Association, Articles of Incorporation, or the Certificate of Incorporation would contain the aforementioned details of the organization. It's important to remember that this document takes precedence over all others, and members of the organization cannot adopt anything that conflicts with this critical document.

Bylaws

Usually referred to as the bylaws, this document does not contain the parliamentary procedure that is the focus of this book but the rules that the organization has to abide by. These bylaws define the organization's nature, its members, meetings, and officers and describe its operation, which is just as important as the corporate charter.

It must be pointed out that these rules are very different from the rules of how to conduct business, even if both are equally important when it comes to conducting business the right way. As mentioned earlier, any business conducted that contradicts the corporate charter, or even the bylaws cannot be adopted. In fact, the bylaws are very much like a constitution and whose laws cannot be changed, not unless a large majority backs a motion to do so. For example, the number of members who set the quorum will be a part of this document, but not in the rules of order.

Rules of Order

If an organization has a corporate charter and bylaws but does not have any rules of order, this can be easily sorted by obtaining a copy of Robert's Rules of Order. Of course, the organization can modify it for their convenience. For example, some motions are debatable, while others aren't. The organization can adopt the rules of order but use it flexibly to impact problem-solving at their meetings.

Depending on the organization's needs, one can tweak which motion is debatable or not and does not have to follow the parliamentary procedures mentioned in the book. For that matter, the order of business that an organization conducts might be very different from the norm. Of course, coming up with new ways to vote, debate, or even preside is unnecessary.

Finally, one must not mix up the bylaws along with the rules of order. It is advisable to include both in the same book, but the members must be informed. This is because the parliamentary procedures adopted can be amended by previous notice and if the amendment receives a two-thirds vote.

Standing Rules

Finally, another set of rules that concern the administration of the organization are called standing rules. To create a standing rule, a main motion needs to be brought at a meeting, and the rule will remain in effect until the assembly decides to do away with or amend the standing rule. One example of this is deciding how to give awards for achievements. Even if these rules do not aid in conducting orderly meetings, these rules, when written down, can help new members understand what needs to be done when faced with certain administrative decisions.

Necessary Documentation For Meetings

Now, while the documents mentioned earlier serve as an excellent foundation to aid members, officers, and committees to conduct business quickly, three other documents are commonly used in meetings that help both members and officers do the same.

Agenda

Almost everyone who has been to a meeting understands the importance of following a particular agenda. A simple definition of an agenda involves a list of action items that need to be completed at the meeting for which it has been prepared. Suppose you're not sure why an agenda helps. Try running a meeting without one. Without a doubt, using an agenda gives the meeting a clear purpose and direction but also saves time.

Apart from the usual benefits, an agenda follows a particular structure derived from the order of business conducted. This could differ from organization to organization and can be obtained from Robert's Rules of Order if not prepared for meetings.

Minutes of Meeting

The Minutes of Meeting is a document that records what happens in the previous meeting before its adjournment. There might be motions that have carried over to this meeting but that are not on the agenda and might have been missed by absent members. Recording the minutes of meeting is important enough because it provides continuity and which is why there is no time limit if corrections need to be made. If one looks at the accepted order of business in Robert's Rules of Order, the minutes of meeting is generally read at the beginning of every meeting and approved before moving on to other items on the agenda.

Reports

Another essential document that is shared is reports by officers, boards, and committees. Not every meeting will include the sharing of a report with the members. However, these documents are just as important as the other two when a deliberative assembly meets. One example of this report includes the treasurer's monthly report on balance, receipts, and expenditures for the organization's activities.

Putting It All Together

Until now, we have looked at the key players in a deliberative assembly and the governing documents. We have also looked at three documents necessary to conduct business as part of a deliberative assembly. Still, our understanding of a deliberative assembly would not be complete without a list of fundamental rules that must be adhered to for a meeting to be considered valid, courteous, and productive.

Every Meeting Must Reach a Quorum

To carry out business, there should be a minimum number of members who have to be present at meetings, which is called the quorum of the assembly. A quorum is considered necessary because business should not be conducted by a minimal number of people present at the meeting. As far as the organization is concerned, this small group of people cannot represent all the absent members. Of course, there are times when people might not be able to make it to a meeting and which is why the bylaws should provide a minimum number of people who can carry out business and represent all those who aren't there. Both the Senate and the House of Representatives require a majority of members present to reach a quorum, but this need not be the same with other types of societies that might adopt Robert's Rules of Order.

Minimum Number of Officers Who Must Preside Over a Meeting

Now, while there is a minimum number of members who must be present at any meeting, two officers must be available to conduct business. The first is a presiding officer who serves as a moderator of the meeting and ensures that the rules are maintained. In addition, a clerk or secretary has to be present as well to make a record of what has been done in the form of minutes of meeting, as discussed earlier.

The presiding officer usually sits at the center of a stage or platform so that the entire hall can see him and vice-versa. Both the individual and the chair that they sit on are referred to as "the chair." The clerk's desk should be placed just next to the presiding officer's chair so that papers can be passed on to the secretary during the meeting efficiently.

How Members Are Expected to Communicate At Each Meeting

The Presiding Officer is referred to as "Mr. President" or "Madam President" and could be either the President or the Vice-President. The term "chairperson," "Chairman," or "chair" is commonly used these days by members to refer to the presiding officer as well. As a rule, members can either only address the chair or address each other through the chair. Other members' names should be avoided. Lastly, it's only when a member has the floor that he can speak but rarely when seated in the deliberative assembly.

How Presiding Officers Are Expected to Communicate at Each Meeting

The Presiding Officer can only refer to himself as "chair," and in the third person. Using the pronoun, "I" is a no-no. In some cases, the presiding officer can use the term "Your President..." but this is when he is speaking in an administrative officer's capacity. The presiding officer is not permitted to use members' names, nor can they refer to them as "You..." except for the time when he or she announces the members of a committee, is assigning the floor to the said member, or participating in a disciplinary procedure.

The Standard "Order of Business" Meetings of a Deliberative Nature

As is the norm, it is the President who will call the meeting to order. This is as soon as he has determined whether a quorum is present, and it is time for the meeting to begin, based on information provided to members who are participating as part of the deliberative assembly. One can find the order of business in the bylaws and which the prepared agenda generally follows. That said, here's an example of the order of business generally adopted by deliberative assemblies of all kinds in meetings:

#1: Reading and Approval of Minutes

#2: Reports of Officers

#3: Reports of Committees (Standing or Special)

#4: Discussion of Special Orders

#5: Unfinished Business & General Orders

#6: New Business

Chapter Summary

- The deliberative assembly is considered a group of people who meet at an agreed time to determine a course of action or conduct business.
- Deliberative assemblies consist of members and officers and consist of five primary types.
- There are four governing documents that members and officers must read before attending meetings: corporate charter, bylaws, rules of order, and standing rules.
- An agenda, minutes of meeting, and officer report are documents used during a meeting.
- A quorum must be reached so that business can be conducted during a meeting while a presiding officer and a clerk must also be present to manage the order of business.
- Both members and presiding officers must refer to each other respectfully and objectively.
- Robert's Rules of Order lists the standard order of business that is conducted in any meeting.

In the next chapter, you will learn more about the different types of meetings.

Chapter Three: About Meetings

Until now, we have looked at the body of people - known as the deliberative assembly - but we have also looked at the governing documents that provide the rules on the rights and duties of members and officers and how they should conduct business by following parliamentary procedure.

The next aspect that should be examined involves the types of meetings usually conducted because it is at these events that business is carried out. In fact, before the meeting takes place, several things need to be put in place. That said, after the meeting is adjourned, it is just as necessary to understand the areas of improvement so that the next meeting can be run better.

So, we will discuss the types of meetings and meeting management and strategies that could prove to be key when preparing for upcoming meetings.

Types of Meetings

But before we get into the types of meetings used by an organization for business, it is best, to begin with, the definition of what a meeting is. By definition, a meeting is nothing but a single gathering of both members and officers of an organization in a specific location to conduct business, with the presence of a quorum. Of course, these members have to be notified with details pertaining to the meeting's date, time, and purpose in advance too. In addition, members remain at the meeting not unless a short recess has been called for, business has been completed, or the members and officers have adjourned the meeting.

Now, there are three types of meetings that usually occur: formal, informal, and electronic meetings. Each of these types of meetings is further subdivided into specific meetings where they have specific requirements.

Formal Meetings

According to Robert's Rules of Order, formal meetings occur in the presence of the entire membership to hear the reports of the board, officers, and committees and conduct business by putting forth motions, discussing or debating them, and voting on these motions. Since this is a book about how to conduct business in an orderly and productive manner, it should be clear that formal meetings require strict adherence to parliamentary procedures on the part of both the members and the officers present.

1. Annual Meetings

These meetings are conducted once a year, but they can also be regular meetings even if they are referred to as an annual meeting in the bylaws. Clearly, if unfinished business remains, it will get carried over to the next annual or regular meeting. Now, since there is a considerable time gap between the two annual meetings, the assembly will refer the business to a committee for it to be carried over to the next annual meeting.

2. Regular Meetings

In stark contrast to an annual meeting, a regular meeting involves the periodic meeting of an assembly weekly, monthly, or quarterly. The bylaws should state the day of the meeting while the standing rules should mention the meeting time. If organizations meet quarterly or much more frequently, motions can be carried over to the next meeting by postponing or reconsidering the motion, laying the motion on the table, or even referring the motion to a committee.

3. Adjourned Meetings

An adjourned meeting is a meeting that has been continued from a previous one since it was not able to finish the business at a regular or special meeting. The new time and place of the adjourned meeting is set by a motion that fixes the time until which to adjourn or by a main motion that adjourns the meeting until a specified time. Of course, in this instance, the minute of meeting taken at the previous meeting is read as part of the order of business and then unfinished, and new business is then taken up before the deliberative assembly.

4. Executive Sessions

In an executive session, only members of the organization are permitted to attend and are, for all practical purposes, closed meetings to everyone else. Apart from assembly meetings, board and committee meetings are considered to be executive sessions. While the latter two types of meetings only involve specific members, assembly meetings can sometimes include guests. Members might not want guests to listen to the discussion taking place and can close off the meeting to these guests by making a motion so that the assembly meeting can go into executive session. Obviously, the business conducted in an executive session has to remain confidential, and the minutes of meeting can only be read in another executive session. Disciplinary action is usually taken up against a member in an executive session.

5. Special Meetings

As expected, a special meeting usually occurs at a time that is distinct from the regular meeting held by said organization. The bylaws should give them details about the time, place, and purpose of the meeting, who can call the special meeting, and why the meeting can be called. Members also have to be notified regarding the business that needs to be discussed before the special meeting occurs. Lastly, the procedure for a special meeting also has to be specified in the bylaws.

6. Sessions

While new and unfinished business comes up in regular meetings, sessions are a series of meetings that take place to deal with just one order of business or program. At the beginning of a new meeting in a session, unfinished business is continued from where it was left off in the prior meeting. Sessions are usually seen in conventions.

7. Conventions

Conventions, being unlike regular meetings, usually consist of delegates picked from units of an organization spread across a large geographical area. Being representatives of these units, they are selected to attend a convention that usually takes place once a year and lasts for about a week. Conventions can also occur more frequently, and this depends on how big the organization is and how much business needs to be conducted. Regardless of which, delegates must meet the credentials committee before they can participate in convention business to receive the documentation that they need to enter the convention floor. As for its order of business, conventions call their order of business a program put together by the program committee. Finally, once a convention wraps up business, it adjourns sine die, which means adjournment without a day. Having said that, the bylaws of any organization should provide all the necessary details regarding how conventions have to be held.

8. Mass Meetings

In stark contrast to an executive session, a mass meeting involves the participation of an unorganized group even if a meeting place and time are provided to bring people together to either form an organization or fix a community issue. Since there are no bylaws, the sponsors can limit the discussion while attendees have the right to make motions, debate, and vote. In particular, the sponsors can eject anyone who tries to oppose or distract others from attaining the mass meeting's purpose. Lastly, if the assembly requires another meeting, the next meeting's details have to be shared before the current meeting is adjourned. Or else, the assembly would be dissolved, and it will be necessary to start all over again if a meeting is called at a later date. That said, for the parliamentary procedure on how to conduct mass meetings, one can use the framework of rules that Robert's Rules of Order offers.

Informal Meetings

Informal meetings differ from formal meetings because they are specifically designed for boards and committees whose membership is under 12. Yet the main reason these meetings are called is that they are informal when it comes to adherence to the rules. Both the members and presiding officers can remain seated, do not have to address the chair, and discuss ideas prior to making a motion. Despite this informality, an agenda still needs to be followed, and the discussion should remain pertinent to the topic allotted for the meeting itself.

1. Board Meetings

Board meetings are not very different from regular meetings in that business must be transacted in a proper meeting. A quorum should be present while members must be notified of the meeting in advance. The secretary must put down the minutes of meeting. Of course, the minutes can only be read by the board members, not unless votes by board members to release the minutes to all members is reached. As for what occurs in a board meeting, it is the duty of the executive committee to report to the board what has taken place since the last board meeting. That said, the formality of the board meeting depends on how small or large the board itself is. Of course, suppose a board meeting becomes chaotic. In that case, the presiding officer can turn the meeting into a formal one by informing the members that parliamentary rules have to be put into place.

2. Committee Meetings

In the case of committee meetings, the chairman of the committee usually calls for a meeting by setting the time, date, and place and notifying all the committee members about it. Committee meetings are called to make certain decisions and recommendations that the assembly will adopt after further discussion and voting is complete. Of course, the committee chairman is appointed by the presiding officer of the assembly or committee members themselves. Still, if a chairman does not call for a meeting, this responsibility can be taken up by two committee members. Operating like a small board, a committee meeting adheres to the same rules and parliamentary procedures created by the organization and used in regular meetings. As always, the will of the committee when it comes to making a decision has to be a majority vote.

Electronic Meetings

Face-to-face meetings are not the only means by which people can assemble these days. In an era where communication methods such as telephone, email, and videoconferencing are available, meetings can be conducted this way too. The bylaws should enable officers and members to assemble in such a manner whenever possible, even if the accepted parliamentary procedure has to be enforced by the presiding officer and followed by the members. Another option that could be used involves email meetings, but this is only if members reside far away from each other. This is because things can get confusing and chaotic if this medium is used to make decisions instead of formally meeting in person. As suggested in Robert's Rules of Order, email is best used to inform people of announcements and meetings and send minutes, reports, and agendas.

A Note on Meeting Management

Meetings do not necessarily meet all goals set. In several situations, meetings lead to more meetings, and this becomes a complete waste of time, especially since nothing gets done. What makes matters worse is that with meetings sometimes going off track or people speaking out of turn, chaos ensues.

So, it becomes difficult for a presiding officer to stay on track with the meeting agenda. Since these issues usually occur in informal meetings, adopting helpful techniques to manage your meetings become necessary. Here are a few tips for just about anyone who wants to conduct an informal meeting but get the necessary results:

- Avoid having a meeting if you can get work done using another method.

- If a meeting is absolutely necessary, reduce the number of attendees and the meeting time. Ensure you only invite people who must be there and give them as much notice as humanly possible. Ensure that you provide all meeting details in the call of the meeting while testing all equipment and presentation material before the meeting occurs.

- Begin the meeting on time.

- Take sufficient time to finish the meeting's objectives but stick to the schedule decided upon. At all times, stick to the agenda and prevent the discussion from straying from the agreed order of business.

- Ensure that someone takes the minutes of the meeting, which includes action items and target dates of completion. Make sure this responsibility is carried out correctly before ending the meeting.

- Understand what your role is as part of this meeting. In other words, you have to be clear about what you are responsible for and the authority that you wield to make key decisions. In preparing the agenda for the meeting, make sure you prepare for the meeting in every way possible.

- Understand when to use general consent instead of a vote when chairing meetings. There are certain items in the agenda that do not require much deliberation and for these items, using general consent saves time. One example of this includes approving the previous minutes of meeting.

- Employ the use of committees so that much more work can be accomplished for the organization.

- If you are assigning work to other people, give them accurate instructions to know what needs to be done.

- Even if you aren't the leader of a meeting, it is your responsibility to make sure that he or she is doing what she is supposed to do. Not only should he or she know what the agenda items are but also what decisions and action plans will be recommended in the meeting. Of course, being impartial but making sure that the discussion adheres to the agenda is the leader's vital responsibility. No matter what, his primary responsibility is to keep the meeting on track.

Chapter Summary

- Organizational meetings consist of three types: formal, informal, and electronic.
- While formal meetings involve the entire membership, informal meetings are usually restricted to a meeting of 12 individuals or lesser.
- The common types of formal meetings are mass, annual, regular, and special meetings, as well as sessions, executive sessions, and conventions.
- Board and committee meetings are the two types of informal meetings.
- Conducting electronic meetings via telephone, videoconferencing and email are acceptable if members live at some distance from each other. However, using email to make key decisions should be avoided as it can waste time and confuse members. Using email to keep members informed of announcements and meeting documentation like the agenda, reports, and minutes is a better way to use this communication method.
- If you are conducting an informal meeting to get work done, it is best to consider a list of techniques that could help you chair or participate in a productive and efficient gathering.

In the next chapter, you will learn about core principles that must be upheld to conduct business in an orderly and productive manner in a deliberative assembly.

Chapter Four: Conducting Business the RRO Way

As we begin Chapter 5, it is time to understand the most basic principles of chairing a meeting in an orderly and productive manner. Now that we know the key players who are part of any meeting, the governing documents that describe how business should be conducted, the standard order of business, and the types of meetings that take place, we have to first look at the most common scenario that describes how business is presented.

In Chapter 3, we saw the most accepted order of business involves reading the minutes of the previous meeting, reading the reports from officers, boards, and committees, and discussing special orders. Of course, unfinished and new business is generally discussed last. One might wonder as to what the nature of this business is? Or how is it presented to both the members and presiding officers in the assembly? Let us look at how business should be ideally conducted in a deliberative assembly, according to Robert's Rules of Order.

It all begins with bringing up motions in front of the assembly for their consideration. Ideas are brought up for discussion and a vote and must be addressed to the chair by a member. Before making a motion, one must be aware of including all the details before bringing it up for the assembly to decide on. Consisting of several types, it is the main motion that is usually considered as unfinished or new business that needs to be debated and voted on even if other types of motions will be discussed in a future chapter. Motions that were not voted upon in a prior meeting are considered unfinished business.

For example, stating a motion occurs by saying: "Mr. President, I move that we purchase office supplies and new computers for a total cost of $2000."

Once this motion is brought up, the chairman will usually repeat it for the benefit of the assembly. After this, the motion that has been brought up has to be seconded by another member present. In most cases, a member will say "Second" or "I second the motion."

If this does happen, then the presiding officer has to restate the motion to the assembly, then members will have to discuss the merits of such a motion. If the motion isn't seconded, then the presiding officer will have to proceed with the next agenda. The presiding officer has to stay impartial here and is not allowed to make any decisions related to the motion placed before the assembly, not unless he vacates his chair to another presiding officer.

When the discussion stage is reached, the person who brought up the motion is given the right to speak first and which involves taking the floor while everyone else is seated. Now, every other member of the assembly also has the right to discuss and debate why this motion is good or bad. They do this by addressing each other through the chair.

Before they begin speaking, each member should state whether they are speaking for or against the motion. Still, whether you are for or against the motion, everyone in the assembly should and will get a chance and which is why members who have finished speaking once usually have to wait their turn for everyone else to do so if they wish to speak again. This discussion of the motion will continue until it is time for the membership to vote for or against the motion. This is usually when none of the members will get up to speak to the motion.

Now, there are several methods by which a vote is taken, and once it is concluded with a clear decision, the president has to announce the results by stating whether the motion is lost or carried. A motion is lost if more than 50% of the membership does not vote for it. If a motion is carried, then the details on how the action pertaining to the motion will have to be carried out have to be announced by the presiding officer.

The presiding officer will announce the results by saying: "The ayes have it, and the motion is carried. We will be purchasing office supplies and new computers for a total cost of $2000."

Lastly, when the vote is a tie, the presiding officer can vote and break the tie if he is a member. However, if the vote is a tie after casting his vote, the motion is considered lost.

What makes parliamentary procedure appealing and fair is what happens when a member doubts the vote. All that any member has to do is use the word "Division," and this results in a retake of the vote by using a different method selected by the chair.

That said, even if this procedure on how to carry out business in a deliberative assembly seems simple enough, there's every chance of the meeting going off track by not sticking to the meeting agenda. Both sides in a debate can use strategies to delay and kill a motion and might be in the best interests of the meeting and the organization itself. So, it is advised that some core principles - based on Robert's Rules of Order - should be remembered by the presiding officer at said meeting. These core principles are not very different from those discussed for informal meetings at the end of Chapter 4.

#1: Taking Up One Business Item at a Time

This is probably the most fundamental principle in parliamentary procedure and involves following the order of business carefully and includes taking up one pending main motion at a time. This keeps things simple. For that matter, secondary motions can be made, but the latter will be given precedence over the former, and they will be discussed one at a time. As you might have also noticed, only one member can be given the floor at once. This is so that confusion can be avoided by staying focused on one agenda item or individual at a time.

#2: Alternation Between Opposite Points of View in Assignment of the Floor

Now, when it is time for the members to speak on the motion made, the presiding officer must alternate between members who are speaking for or against the motion when assigning the floor to them. As a result, both sides of the debate are heard equally and require the presiding officer to be impartial to carry this out properly. One must remember that the discussion before the vote usually helps members decide which way they're going to go when it is time to vote, so both sides of the debate should be heard.

#3: Requirement that the Chair Always Calls for the Negative Vote

Except for non-controversial motions, the chair or the presiding officer must always call for the negative vote after asking for the affirmative vote first. This is despite the scenario in which the affirmative vote has backed the motion unanimously. One must remember that while the majority does rule, the rights and voice of the minority also have to be heard.

#4: Decorum and Avoidance of Personalities in Debate

As most experienced debaters would know, there are times when being courteous and objective becomes difficult, especially when we are losing a debate. This is why members must maintain decorum by addressing each other through the chair and avoiding crosstalk at all costs, particularly when they do not agree with others on said motion. In fact, they are required to refer to each other in an objective manner, referring to each other in the third person. Suppose passions arise, and this rule is not adhered to. In that case, there is every chance that name-calling and violent behavior can destroy the deliberative assembly's purpose.

#5: Confinement of Debate to the Merits of the Pending Question

It is the will of both the members and the presiding officers to have a productive and orderly meeting. In most cases, parliamentary rules usually limit each member's speech to a particular time limit - say ten minutes in all. This ensures that everyone gets heard during the meeting and helps members avoid diverging from the pending question. No matter what, the time that is allotted to members to speak should focus solely on the motion's merits and nothing else. There can be no personal attacks made either. In this case, the presiding officer has to end a speech that is not related to the motion put forth in front of the assembly.

#6: Division of a Question

Finally, if there are parts of a motion with numerous questions or topics, it's possible that the assembly supports one question or topic but does not back the other. So, in this case, the members can request a division of the question to separate these parts of the main motion and vote on them separately. In using the example provided on how to state the main motion in a deliberative assembly, if the assembly wanted to service the computers but did not want to spend money on office supplies, both of these parts could be split into two separate motions. Both of these questions could then be voted on separately to decide a course of action on separated questions.

Chapter Summary

- Business is conducted by making a motion in the assembly. This could be either unfinished business from a previous meeting or new business altogether.
- After the motion is presented, the members debate and discuss its merits by taking the floor, one person at a time. They address the chair directly or each other through the chair.
- Once no one wishes to debate the issue, a vote is taken to decide whether the vote is carried or lost. If it is the former, the presiding officer will also have to determine how the action pertaining to the motion should be carried out.
- Not every meeting goes according to the agenda, so presiding officers must remember core principles when chairing a meeting the RRO way.
- Taking up one business item at a time, keeping the discussion on the point, always calling for the negative vote, maintaining decorum, splitting a motion into parts, and hearing both sides of the debate equally are core principles that are worth adopting in any formal meeting.

In the next chapter, you will learn everything you need to know about motions.

Chapter Five: Everything You Need to Know About Motions

In describing how a deliberative assembly must conduct business, we've already discussed how to do so using a main motion. However, other types of motions, known as secondary motions, either support the main motion or choose another course of action in the end.

In this chapter, we will look at motions in much greater detail. Understanding how to use motions is key to getting things done in an assembly. For a start, let us look at eight characteristics to define a motion in much greater detail. In doing this, you will understand the classes of motions better that will be discussed after this.

Eight Characteristics of Motions

Based on our understanding of motions so far, there are main motions. However, secondary motions also exist. Both these motions discussed have certain characteristics that must be understood so that each of them can be used effectively in a deliberative assembly. Comparing what these secondary motions share in common with or differ from main motions can help understand what motions are on the whole.

#1: Over which motions are said motion more important? What motions do said motion yield to? For example, the main motion ranks lowest when it comes to importance and yields to all other motions.

#2: Which motions or situations is said motion applicable to? Subsidiary and some incidental motions apply to the main motion, but the reverse isn't necessarily true.

#3: Is said motion in order while another has the floor? A main motion is set aside temporarily when a secondary motion is placed before the assembly for consideration.

#4: Does said motion require a member to second it? A main motion requires a second while the call for order of the day motion does not.

#5: Can the assembly debate on the said motion? While a main motion is debatable, the Lay on the Table motion is not.

#6: Is said motion amendable? While a main motion is amendable, the Previous Question motion is not.

#7: What vote is necessary for the motion to be adopted? The main motion normally requires a majority vote, but a two-thirds vote must be obtained for the limit or extend the limits of debate.

#8: Can the aid motion be reconsidered? A main motion can be reconsidered while the Lay on the Table motion cannot.

Having discussed the characteristics of a motion, let us define and understand the main motion.

The Main Motion

As we know by now, the main motion is used by members of the assembly to introduce business for its consideration. Up until the chairman restates the business to the assembly, the one who introduced the motion is considered to be its owner and can choose to either withdraw or revise it. However, once it is placed before the assembly, the motion can be amended, delayed, or killed to suit the will of the majority. The assembly is now the joint owner of the motion and must decide what action needs to be taken for a motion that could affect the assembly as a whole. In the example used in an earlier chapter, the assembly has to decide whether $2000 should be spent to buy office supplies and new computers as this action will affect its budget on the whole.

Now, there is another type of main motion - called the incidental main motion - that does not introduce new business but seeks to iron out the details related to the motion's procedure. For example, if the main motion states that $2000 needs to be spent to buy office supplies and new computers, the incidental main motion is approved by the assembly. The term 'incidental' refers to the motion being related to the main motion and from which it has been created to conduct business in an orderly fashion.

Secondary Motions

Not very differently, secondary motions can be brought before the assembly and which are directly related to the main motion. While they have to be introduced by a member and seconded by another, their introduction helps the assembly decide what to do with the main motion or how to conduct business itself. As soon as the secondary motion is introduced after the main motion, it immediately becomes the pending motion and has to be dealt with first. Despite two motions pending, the assembly takes one item of business at a time because of the importance assigned to each of them.

There are three classes of secondary motions, such as the subsidiary, privileged and incidental motions, which need to be discussed given that each of these secondary motions is ranked high or low in terms of their importance to decision-making in the assembly.

Subsidiary Motions

Subsidiary motions help the assembly decide what needs to be done with the main motion that is pending. If you adopt a subsidiary motion, it is going to perform an action on the main motion.

Now, there's a ranking assigned to all subsidiary motions, with Lay on the Table being the highest and Postpone Indefinitely being the lowest. This is for the purpose of the assembly to take up one business item at a time. Consisting of seven motions, let us look at each motion, and what they will do to the main motion they are related to, in their decreasing order of importance:

#1: Lay on the Table means that the main motion will be set aside temporarily.

#2: Previous Question means that debate on the main motion has to be stopped immediately.

#3: Limit or Extend Limits of Debate will shorten or lengthen the debate on a main motion currently pending.

#4: The Postpone to a Certain Time motion will put off the main motion to be dealt with at another time.

#5: The Refer to a Committee motion will delegate the investigation of the main motion to an appointed committee.

#6: The Amend motion will alter it to be much more acceptable for the membership to debate and vote on.

#7: Finally, the Postpone Indefinitely motion will kill a motion for good.

These subsidiary motions have been presented so that the most important is discussed first just so that one keeps track of the order of importance when using it to conduct business at an assembly.

Of course, this list of motions that are ranked would not be complete without addressing the privileged motions that comprise a second-ranked class of motions.

Privileged Motions

Privileged motions do not have anything to do with the business being conducted in the assembly. Instead, they deal with particular matters that have to be dealt with immediately and without debate. So, it should be obvious that privileged motions are ranked higher in importance compared to subsidiary motions. But that's not all: among the five privileged motions, there is a ranking that must be adhered to. So, let us look at these privileged motions in their decreasing order of importance:

#1: The Fix the Time to Which to Adjourn motion is the highest and involves setting the time when the meeting should be continued.

#2: The Adjourn motion calls for the end of the meeting currently in progress.

#3: The Recess motion, when addressed, allows members to take a break and then return to the place of meeting to continue conducting business.

#4: The Raise a Question of Privilege motion is generally introduced when the right or privilege of the assembly is either diminished in some capacity or requires immediate intervention. In this case, the motion currently pending is interrupted if the chair decides that the motion should be admitted as a question of privilege.

#5: The Call for Orders of the Day motion can be called for by a single member if he or she feels as if the adopted order of business is not being followed. In doing so, the agreed-upon schedule for the day can be enforced, not unless the assembly itself decides not to adhere to the order of business by a two-thirds majority vote.

Incidental Motions

Incidental Motions, while looking to handle questions related to the procedure of pending business, do not affect the pending motion itself. Given the nature of these motions, they are not debatable and have no rank because they are dealt with as soon as they are made. So, let's look at some of the incidental motions that usually come up in a deliberative assembly:

#1: The Point of Order motion informs the presiding officer that he or she is failing to enforce the rules so that he or she can make a ruling immediately. For example, a member can make a point of order if the chair has failed to check if a quorum is present or not.

#2: The Appeal motion comes up when a member disagrees with the chair's ruling on a particular question pertaining to parliamentary procedure. If a member makes an appeal and is seconded by another, then the chair will have to submit this matter on a vote made by the entire assembly.

#3: If a member believes that it would prove harmful even to discuss such a main motion, the motion Objection to the Consideration of the Question can be made by a member. But this has to be made prior to the beginning of the debate or to making a subsidiary motion related to the main motion.

#4: If the main motion is in written form or a resolution containing several paragraphs and sections, each paragraph or section can be amended exclusively by proposing the motion Consideration by Paragraph or Seriatim.

#5: If a member doubts the final result of the voice vote or one that requires a show of hands or doubts that the minimum number of representatives have voted, he can call for a Division of the Assembly motion. The chair has to reconfirm the result by a standing vote.

#6: If a division of the assembly has resulted in an inconclusive vote, a member can make a motion so that a vote can be taken either by ballot, roll call, or by a counted standing vote. This motion can also call for the closing or reopening of a ballot vote.

#7: If the organization's bylaws do not explain how nominations are to be made, a member can specify how a nomination can take place or even close or reopen nominations. This is only if the election is still pending, and the assembly has not taken any action just yet.

#8: If a member wishes to be relieved of duty placed on him either by the office that he or she holds or by the bylaws, then the Request to be Excused from Duty motion can be used to do so.

#9: Parliamentary inquiry, Request for Information, Request for Permission, Request to Read Papers, and Request for any other

Privilege are a list of inquiries and requests that can be made and which pertains to pending or finished business.

#10: In some cases, the assembly might decide on a course of action or discuss a question that might violate a rule. For this, the Suspend the Rules motion can temporarily bypass the rules so that business can be conducted.

#11: If a motion consists of two or more parts that can be split into two further motions, the assembly can put both questions to a separate vote. This is only possible if a member makes the motion for a Division of the Question.

Motions that Bring a Question Again Before the Assembly

Now, along with main and secondary motions, there is another type of motion that helps to bring back motions for consideration before the assembly. Of course, to make such a motion, all pending motions must be resolved.

For example, if a motion was set aside temporarily, it can be brought back by the Take from the Table motion. If members are not pleased with prior action at a previous meeting, then rescinding the action or amending something previously adopted is also possible. Discharging a committee is also another motion that belongs to this category. That said, except for the Take from the Table motion, all the others need to be seconded, are debatable, and must obtain a two-thirds vote for the motion to carry.

A Note on the Ranking of Motions

As we close this chapter, we need to reemphasize one principle that involves taking one item of business at a time. For this very reason, the main, subsidiary, and privileged motions all have to be ranked in such a manner that the assembly can carry out business in an orderly and productive manner.

For starters, the main motion is the lowest-ranked motion in this list, following which subsidiary motions are given more importance. As the term suggests, privileged motions enjoy the highest priority when you club all these motions together. In other words, the motion to adjourn a meeting will take precedence over the motion to amend a main motion. Also, fixing the time until which to adjourn enjoys the highest rank while the main motion, rather ironically, is the least important.

This brings us to the aspects of making and voting on motions in a meeting. Members can only make motions that are much more important than the pending motion. For example, it is fine for members to request a recess if the pending motion involves the discussion of whether to refer the main motion to a committee or not.

Alternatively, if the Previous Question motion is the pending motion, you will not make the Postpone Indefinitely motion. However, when it comes to voting on the pending motions for that meeting, the most critical motions have to be voted on before moving on to a less important one discussed in that meeting.

As one might imagine, the main motion will usually be the last motion to be voted on unless there are no secondary motions placed before the assembly. Adhering to this pattern of how motions are made and voted on will ensure that you stay on point when following parliamentary procedure at said meeting.

Chapter Summary

- Motions are used to conduct business.
- Motions consist of main and secondary motions.
- For those interested in adopting parliamentary procedure, understanding the eight characteristics of a motion is important.
- Secondary motions consist of subsidiary, privileged, and incidental motions.
- Another class of motions that brings back an earlier motion before the assembly also exists.
- Subsidiary and some incidental motions are related to the pending main motion, while privileged motions pertain to the process of carrying out business at said meeting.
- Along with the main motion, privileged and subsidiary motions are assigned a rank while incidental motions, being procedural in nature, are not. This is to help members make a motion or vote on one in the right order.

In the next chapter, you will learn about participating in debates in a respectful and objective manner.

Chapter Six: Participating Courteously and Objectively in Debates

It should be clear that introducing business involves placing a motion before the deliberative assembly by the chair. Yet voting on such a motion immediately does not make sense since every member has the right to understand what this new business is. Upon doing so, each member also has the right to then consider the right course of action according to his or her point-of-view and then cast his or her vote.

In doing so, the assembly, as a whole, will make an informed decision based on the facts surrounding the motion and which are usually presented by the members after the chair places the motion before the assembly. No matter what, it is advisable not to avoid any discussion or debate regarding a motion just so that time can be saved or the opposition can be silenced.

In fact, the act of debating or discussing a motion is so important that the chair cannot move on to taking a vote, not unless all members who wish to speak on the motion's merits have done so. Of course, the assembly itself can pass a motion to limit or close debate, but that still requires a two-thirds majority.

Rules Related to Assigning the Floor to a Member

Any member in the assembly has the right to make a motion or offer his take on said motion by joining the debate. To do this, he must first rise and address the chair, who will then recognize his right to seek the floor. This is done by announcing the person's title and place, which means that the floor is now his to use for said purpose. For that matter, the member can begin debating on the pending motion while suggesting a secondary motion prior to completing his allotted time on the floor. In smaller meetings, the chair will simply nod to the member to indicate that he or she has been assigned the floor.

Now, there are situations in which two members might rise to obtain recognition to use the floor for whatever purpose. When the debatable question is immediately pending, the member who made the motion gets to speak first. Also, no member who has taken the floor to speak can do so again on the same day unless all the members have spoken.

In the case where the question raised is undebatable, the floor can only be given to a member who wants to give previous notice of a motion, make a motion or raise a question that ranks much higher in importance to the immediately pending question.

In the situation where there is no question pending, and a member has risen to make a main motion, another member will be given preference if he wishes to reconsider and Enter on the Minutes, move to reconsider a vote, call up a motion to Reconsider that has been made earlier, give previous notice or move to take a question from the table.

Lastly, if the chair is not sure about who to give the floor to, a vote can decide who gets the floor by virtue of winning the largest number of votes. Of course, if the chair makes a mistake in assigning the floor to a wrong person, a Point of Order can be raised to make a correction.

Rules of Debate

Even if we've already established that every member can debate, the privileges given to members in this regard still involve adhering to the established parliamentary rules. So, here are some rules of debate that are considered mandatory:

#1: Members cannot debate while being seated. They have to be officially recognized by the chair and should be assigned the floor for this purpose.

#2: The member who made the motion is given the right to speak first on the motion and can do so after the chair has placed the motion for the assembly to deliberate on.

#3: As mentioned earlier, members can only speak twice if everyone else has completed speaking on the same day. If the meeting is continued to another day, his right to debate is reset.

#4: Each member is allowed to speak for ten minutes unless the assembly has decided on another amount of time.

#5: The debate has to be relevant to the motion.

#6: Debaters or speakers must address remarks to the chair while avoiding crosstalk at all costs.

#7: Speakers must remain courteous while avoiding personal attacks or questioning members' motives in their remarks. Profanity is a no-no.

#8: Speakers have to refer to officers by title but refrain from using other members' names.

#9: When debating on a motion, it is essential to let the assembly know which side of the issue he or she is on. For example, the member can say: "I speak for [or against] the motion because..." In fact, the presiding officer can ask: "Would someone like to speak in favor [or against] the motion?" This helps the presiding officer alternate between points of view when assigning the floor to the next member.

#10: Members cannot debate against their own motion, but they can vote against it. However, the person who seconds the motion can speak against it.

#11: Members should not disturb the assembly during the debate by whispering, walking across the floor, talking, or using other forms of distractions.

#12: While a member has been assigned the floor for debate, the presiding officer has to remain seated or stand back in such a way that the assembly can see him or her.

#13: The presiding officer can interrupt the speaker for a ruling or provide information and during which the member has to be seated until the officer finishes. Once he or she is done, the member can then rise again to continue the debate.

#14: Members cannot give their time from the debate time allotted to them to other members who are speaking on the same side of the issue. The unused portion of the ten minutes allotted is lost if the member does not use it wisely.

#15: The presiding officer must also remain impartial during the debate even if he is a member. If he does wish to speak, then he will have to relinquish the chair to another officer before doing so. He or she can resume the chair once the motion has been put to a vote or has been temporarily set aside.

Debatable and Non Debatable Motions

As mentioned in the previous chapter, knowing which motions are debatable and those that cannot help when serving as a member in a deliberative assembly.

For this purpose, it is good to know that two subsidiary motions are considered debatable while the rest are not. All privileged motions are considered undebatable. Lastly, all but two incidental motions are undebatable.

For more detail, here is a list of debatable and non-debatable motions.

Debatable Motions

- Main motion
- Postpone Indefinitely
- Amend
- Refer to a committee
- Postpone to a certain time
- Appeal from the decision of the chair
- Rescind
- Amend something previously adopted
- Reconsider
- Recess (as an incidental main motion)
- Fix the time to which to adjourn (as an incidental main motion)

Undebatable Motions

- Limit or extend the limits of debate
- Previous Question
- Lay on the table
- Take from the Table
- Call for orders of the day
- Raise a question of privilege
- Recess (as a privileged motion)
- Adjourn
- Fix the time to which to adjourn (as a privileged motion)
- Point of order
- Withdraw a motion
- Suspend the rules
- Object to consideration of the motion
- Division of the assembly
- Division of the question
- Incidental motions related to voting, when the subject is pending
- Dispense with the reading of the minutes

Chapter Summary

- Every member has the privilege of participating in debate but should do it in accordance with the accepted parliamentary procedure in place.
- Debates should not be avoided to save time or silence the opposition.
- A member should rise and address the chair first in order to be recognized and given the floor to debate or speak.
- The chair will mention the person's title and place in order to assign him or her the floor to speak or debate.
- Members can speak to serve multiple purposes. For example, debate on one motion and then suggest a secondary motion.
- Members can rise simultaneously to be assigned to the floor. There are particular rules by which preference is given to a said member, but in the case of indecision, a vote can be cast in the assembly to decide.
- There are basic rules of debate that must be adhered to by all members and officers. For this book, we have chosen the best 15 rules.
- Knowing which motions are debatable and undebatable is important to participate in the proceedings of a deliberative assembly. For this book, we have listed both the debatable and undebatable motions.

In the next chapter, you will learn about the different voting methods and the importance of the majority vote in a deliberative assembly.

Chapter Seven: All About Voting

In the previous chapter, we looked at a member's right to speak or debate on an issue put forth to the assembly. The decision taken after the members decide to stop debating can affect the assembly significantly, so it is absolutely necessary that every present member casts their vote. Of course, the democratic way is for one person to cast only one vote regarding a single course of action.

Now, there are a number of ways by which votes are cast, be it by voice, roll call, by rising, or even by a show of hands. These are the most common methods. However, in certain situations, members do not even have to be physically present in order to cast their vote. They can also send their vote well in advance by mail or by email, telephone, or video conferencing. However, provisions in the bylaws have to be made for voting methods that are not considered common.

Regardless of which, reaching a decision by obtaining a majority of votes is a democratic principle that will never go out of fashion. For some decisions, a two-thirds or three-fourths vote is necessary. It's simple, really. The majority's will is the will of the entire assembly, even if the minority has to accept graciously that their decision was not necessarily the most popular course of action.

Now, since this book focuses on parliamentary procedure for a deliberative assembly, it makes sense to begin this chapter by covering the procedure for voting.

Procedure for Taking a Vote

Since the presiding officer is tasked with maintaining order in a meeting, it should come as no surprise that his or her role in the voting procedure is crucial.

#1: The chair should ask for the affirmative vote first, and then the negative vote, no matter how unanimous the affirmative vote seems. Staying neutral is important, too, to ensure that a fair vote was taken. For example, the chair can say: "The question is on buying office supplies and new computers for $2000. All those in favor say 'Aye'. All those opposed say 'Nay'."

#2: The chair should not ask for abstentions or count the number of people who abstained from voting as this has no bearing on the results.

#3: The chair should announce the results of the vote and whether the motion is lost or carried. If the affirmative vote is greater, then the chair should also state who will carry out the course of action. A motion made by the members will determine who should carry out the action if the chair has no idea. Or else, the presiding officer states: "The noes have it. The motion is lost, and we will not purchase office supplies and new computers for $2000. Is there any further business?"

#4: The presence of a quorum is mandatory during a vote, and the chair must be aware of this before the meeting begins.

#5: While the chair can retake the vote using another method, if they doubt the result, a member can do the same by saying "Division". If this happens in the case of a roll call or ballot vote, the votes will have to be recounted. Verifying a vote is absolutely necessary if either a member or the chair has doubts about the decisiveness of the vote taken.

Rules of Voting

Now, there are certain rules that every member should adhere to when it comes to voting in a deliberative assembly:

#1: Each member is allowed a maximum of one vote per question or motion. No one else can use that member's vote.

#2: Every member has the right to abstain from voting on said motion. It is not mandatory that members vote for every motion if present in a deliberative assembly.

#3: Members are not allowed to vote on a question of direct personal interest. For example, if a motion states that the organization should sign a commercial contract that benefits one of the members financially, then that member should refrain from voting.

#4: Alternatively, if there's a motion whose decision affects a member in any other way - if said member is running for office - then the member will be allowed to vote as part of the proceedings.

#5: Interruptions are not allowed during a vote except for the time before any member has voted. Or in the case of ballot voting, where other business is usually conducted while the votes are taken or being tabulated.

#6: Members are not allowed to explain why they voted for or against the motion, as this is something that is usually done when debate occurs.

#7: Members are allowed to change their vote only until the time the result has been announced. After this, he can only alter the vote by taking the unanimous consent of the assembly. However, in the case of the latter, this has to be done immediately after the chair has announced the results of the vote.

#8: Members can request or demand certain changes that can affect the overall result itself even after the chair has announced the results of the vote. Except for a point of order, if any proposed action requires one to apply the vote after the results have been announced, it has to be done immediately after the chair has done so or prior to the commencement of a debate or new business.

#9: The assembly plays a prominent role when it comes to judging all questions related to voting or the counting of votes, especially in a situation where uncertainty exists.

The Importance of the Majority Vote

In a democracy, the will of the majority is accepted even if the rights of the minority are also heard. The parliamentary procedure applies this fundamental democratic principle in practice. As we already know, business can only be conducted if a quorum exists and if a majority has voted for said motions. However, some moderately important motions require a majority vote, while others that are far more impactful require a two-thirds or three-fourths vote. Hence, we must understand what these terms mean.

Majority Vote

By definition, a majority vote simply means that more than half of those present at a meeting must vote in favor of the motion. Abstentions or blank ballots are not counted against the motion because only those voting are considered to be present.

While this definition seems simple enough, there are times when organizational bylaws modify their definition of what a majority means when it comes to voting. If a motion requires a majority of those present, then if the results of a vote for a motion is greater than 50% of those present, it is said to qualify as a majority vote. If the organization wants a majority of the membership to vote, regardless of who is present or absent at the meeting, then if the vote taken is greater than 50% of all members, it is said to have qualified as a majority vote. Since these two modifications mean very different things, it is important that this should be stated for the members' benefits in the bylaws.

Two-Thirds Vote

As mentioned earlier, certain motions require a two-thirds vote in favor of a motion. This amounts to two-thirds or more of the members voting for the motion, usually taken by a rising vote. If in doubt of the results, the chair should count those voting on the motion. Limiting or closing debate as well as preventing the introduction of a motion are two motions that require a two-thirds vote.

Three-Fourths Vote

Some organizations prefer a three-fourths vote where three-fourths of the membership has to vote in favor of a motion because of its impact on the organization itself. It's clear that most people should agree to such a motion. A couple of instances where this applies is when officers are elected, or member applications are accepted.

The Tie Vote

When a vote is tied, the result is inconclusive because 50% of the members have voted for the motion, while 50% is against it. A decision cannot be made, which is why this is unacceptable. If no method is available to break this tie, the motion is then deemed lost. As mentioned in an earlier chapter, the presiding officer can break the tie but cannot vote both as an officer and a member. He or she only gets to use one vote. If the officer's vote brings about a tie in the vote, then the motion is considered lost.

Methods of Voting

There are three main methods of voting:

#1: By Voice (or Viva Voce)

This method is generally opted for first when voting on a motion and which involves either stating Aye or Nay for said motion.

#2: By Rising

If the voice vote is inconclusive or the motion requires a two-thirds majority, members can rise either in favor or against the motion placed before the assembly.

#3: By a Show of Hands

Instead of rising, a show of hands either for or against the motion is another method that can be used. This is particularly useful in deliberative assemblies that are small.

Other Voting Methods

#1: By Ballot

For the ballot vote, the members, as well as the presiding officer, both get to vote, unless the organization has a different rule. If there is a ballot box, it is the chair's responsibility to instruct the members to put their ballots in the box. After all the votes are placed, the teller's committee counts the ballots and writes down the result on a teller's sheet. The presiding officer obtains the teller's report and reads it to the membership. Also, there is an option to use electronic devices instead of paper ballots to vote secretly.

#2: By General or Unanimous Consent

If a vote is taken by unanimous consent, it involves handling business for which there will be no objection from the opposition. Paying the bills or leaving the room for a short recess are two excellent examples of this. The chair asks if there is any objection to the motion and, upon hearing none, will declare the motion as carried. If the chair does hear an objection, the motion will be put to the vote.

#3: By Mail/Email

This voting method is generally used by members for whom it is not possible to be physically present at a meeting, but their vote is necessary for important issues such as electing officers or even changing the bylaws. In order for the result of the vote to be conclusive, an accurate mailing list of official members must be furnished to the official sending out the ballots. Of course, this very same voting system can be adapted to email where the official in charge has to request a return receipt from all recipients. The only shortcoming is that it isn't possible to have a secret vote because the official will know how each member voted.

#4: By Roll-Call

Not very differently from a voice vote, the secretary of the meeting calls each member's name in alphabetical order and to which that member should respond, saying "Aye" or "Nay." The presiding officer's name is called last only if his vote can affect the result. Upon obtaining an answer from each member, the secretary repeats the member's name and vote and puts it down in the roll call.

#5: Proxy Voting

In the case of proxy voting, a power of attorney is given to another person who can vote in his stead. While this aspect is not common in deliberative assemblies, a provision in the bylaws can be made.

Chapter Summary

- The presiding officer must call for both the affirmative and negative vote while remaining neutral. The chair must announce the results of the vote and what must be done if the motion is carried.
- Doubting the results of a vote both by the chair and a member can result in retaking the vote by a different method or recounting the vote.
- Each member gets only one vote and can abstain from voting but is not allowed to vote when a motion benefits them directly. If a member is standing for office, he can vote. Members can change their votes but are not allowed to explain their votes to others.
- In a democratic organization, the will of the majority determines the course of action. However, there are variations of the term 'majority,' which can mean very different things when it is time to declare the vote results.
- Some motions are so important that a mere majority does not suffice, but a two-thirds or a three-fourths vote needs to be satisfied.
- In the case of a tie vote, the presiding officer can cast his vote to decide the result but does not get two votes, as a member and an officer. If he or she ties the vote, then the motion is deemed lost.
- There are three common methods of casting a vote: by voice, by rising, and by show of hands.
- Other voting methods include ballot, general or unanimous consent, by mail or email, by roll-call, or by proxy.

In the next chapter, you will implement these principles in an actual walkthrough that conducts the order of business in a deliberative assembly.

Chapter Eight: Implementing RRO in a Meeting

In the chapter on the deliberative assembly, we discussed the order of business generally followed for formal meetings. In this chapter, we will look at a mock scenario using suitable examples along with the statements used by officers and members to ensure that business is conducted in an orderly and productive manner.

Right at the beginning of the meeting, the presiding officer - the President - will call the meeting to order, saying: "The meeting will come to order." [along with one rap of the gavel]

Upon hearing this, members should take their seats based on the request of the presiding officer.

#1: Reading and Approval of Minutes

Since the first order of business involves reading and approving the minutes of the previous meeting, the presiding officer will then say: "Will the secretary read the minutes of the previous meeting?"

Upon saying so, the presiding officer will then take his seat and wait for the secretary or clerk to stand up and read the minutes.

Once the secretary has completed reading the minutes of meeting, the presiding officer will ask: "Are there any corrections?"

If a member believes that a point needed to be added, the presiding officer will ask: "If there is no objection, the minutes will be corrected by adding Daniel's name to the minutes. Are there any further corrections?"

If there are no more corrections to be added, the presiding officer will say: "The minutes are approved as corrected."

#2: Reports of Officers

The next order of business involves hearing the reports of officers and committees. Hence, the presiding officer will state: "The next order of business is the reports of officers. May we have the treasurer's report?"

The treasurer then stands up and reads the report as prepared. Once the report is read, the presiding officer then takes his place and asks: "Are there any questions?"

If there is a question about the treasury report, the presiding officer will redirect the officer's question and then step aside. After the treasurer completes his response, the presiding officer asks: "Are there any other questions? If not, then the treasurer's report is filed."

One must know that said officer's report must be filed with the secretary and does not have to be approved by the assembly. Still, since the treasurer's report is audited, the auditor's report is adopted by the assembly.

#3: Reports of Committees

There are two types of committees where the first gives information about what the said committee has been doing. The second asks members to decide a question and then adds a motion at the end of the report.

The presiding officer says: "The next business in order involves hearing the reports of committees. Will the program committee report?"

The committee chairman will take his place and provide information about the programs that are slated for 2020.

Once the committee chairman has completed making his report, the presiding officer will ask: "Are there any questions?"

If there are no questions by members, the presiding officer will ask: "The program committee's report is filed."

That said, if the program committee wishes to make a recommendation, they can add it to the end of the report and which can be placed before the assembly as a motion for discussion and to be voted on. If the members vote for the motion, the action can then be carried out.

Now, this procedure applies to that of special committees too. The reports of special committees are usually heard at a formal meeting, given that they are created for a specific purpose. That said, once these special committees make their final report, they cease to exist.

#4: Discussion of Special Orders

Special orders are, by definition, motions that have been postponed to the next meeting but have been voted by a two-thirds majority to be considered as such. The main reason why these special orders are voted for is that the assembly deems it necessary to discuss these motions before unfinished business or general orders. Some special orders involve business that occurs annually - say nominations and elections. That said, the parliamentary procedure to introduce and discuss these motions is very similar to that of unfinished business and general orders.

#5: Unfinished Business & General Orders

As the term suggests, unfinished business is a motion that was being discussed when the previous meeting was adjourned. If a motion, much like the one to purchase new computers and office supplies for a total cost of $2000, were voted for in the affirmative, it wouldn't need to be brought up anymore.

On the other hand, general orders involve motions that were postponed to the next meeting but do not enjoy a special order status. It is now time to continue this discussion, but the presiding officer must already know what motions were carried over from previous meetings if they were mentioned on the agenda.

The presiding officer begins by saying: "The next business in order is unfinished business. At the last meeting, a motion to refurbish our London office was postponed to this meeting. Is there any discussion?"

Members will then continue to look at the motion in detail, discuss, and then vote on whether to refurbish the London office or not.

#6: New Business

If there is no unfinished business or general orders, it is time to attend to new business. In some cases, new business is mentioned on the agenda.

If new business isn't on the agenda, the presiding officer will ask: "Is there any new business?"

Or, if it is on the agenda, the presiding officer can state the question and ask what the members want to do. If the members wish to take action, a motion can be made, and then discussion, debate, and the vote can be cast. Or else, if no member wants to take any action, they remain silent.

After completing the discussion of a question or motion, the presiding officer should ask: "Is there any further business?" In fact, the presiding officer has to continue asking this question until no member gets up to make a motion.

If no one rises, the presiding officer has to say: "If there is no objection, the meeting will now adjourn."

If no objection is heard, the presiding officer will finally say: "Since there is no objection, the meeting is adjourned." [along with one rap of the gavel]

Upon saying that, and with the order of business as in the agenda all complete, the meeting is now deemed finished.

Chapter Summary

- The presiding officer calls the order to business, and members have to be seated.
- The secretary reads the minutes of meeting, and the members have to make corrections or approve the minutes.
- Officer and Committee Reports are read next and which are filed with the secretary upon completion.
- Special orders are those that are voted by a two-thirds majority to be deemed so that they are discussed before general orders and unfinished business.
- Speaking of which, general orders and unfinished business are motions that usually carried over from the previous meeting.
- New business can be found on the agenda or otherwise. If it is on the agenda, then the presiding officer should state it. Or ask if any new business is on the agenda.
- Lastly, the meeting is brought to a close by the presiding officer if there is no more new business or objections to the adjournment's announcement.

Final Words

If you have no idea how to conduct a meeting in an orderly and productive manner, this book is precisely what you need since it is based on Robert's Rules of Order. Henry Robert himself faced a similar situation and had to slowly piece together what we now consider a seminal work on the subject of parliamentary procedure. This is his life's work and should be lauded for offering much detail into how meetings are run.

Speaking of which, in an attempt to give readers a hands-on feel of how meetings are conducted, it was necessary to state the guidelines involving the core actions taken in a said meeting and provide a walkthrough of events by following the conventional order of business. Still, there's so much detail to be discovered about motions, members, officers, debating, and voting that are vital aspects of parliamentary procedure that organizations still have questions that need answering.

So, as you use this book as a springboard to bring order and productivity to your organization's meetings, you must understand that Robert's vision to offer a framework of rules that suited non-legislative organizations was also balanced with the understanding that organizations require unique and special rules that might not be part of Robert's work. Feel free to use both in the best interests of your organization. Having said that, think of this book as a guide rather than an instruction manual. Happy reading!

Lightning Source UK Ltd.
Milton Keynes UK
UKHW020703070922
408471UK00010B/942